BLESSED REJECTION

Latoya Williams

CONTENTS

Foreword

Acknowledgements

Introduction

PART I   Family Rejection

PART II   Social Rejection

PART III   Romantic Rejection

PART IV   Blessed Rejection

Dedication

I dedicate this book to the El-Shaddai, God Almighty. Without Him I am nobody, but with Him I am everything.

I dedicate this book to my family, who has been my strength and support system.

I dedicate this book to Leah, a strong woman of God, who through rejection and struggle has taught me that looking for love in all the wrong places is not what was intended for my life and once I totally gave it to Him, He provided ETERNAL SATISFACTION!!!!!!

(Genesis 27-33)

Foreword

I would like to say this is an honor to write the foreword in a book that I know has come from the heart of a young lady that has walked this journey to help inspire, encourage, and motivate others that may have traveled this road or are already on this path. This book entitled, Blessed Rejection, flows from the heart of a young lady who has experienced and seized the moment of being birthed through rejection. When we look at scripture Romans 8:28, "All things" work together for good to them that love God, to them who are called according to His purpose. When reading Blessed Rejection you will go on a journey through the life and eyes of rejection and learn how God will take the very thing that was designed to stop, hinder and destroy you, and make it the biggest and greatest blessing for your life. This book was a definite need to come from the life of Latoya Williams to help others that face rejection from a child into their adult life, so they would be able to understand that God can take all of the no's, you are not worthy enough's, you are not smart enough's, you are not pretty enough's and thrust you into your God given destiny. Blessed Rejection has been written to let you know there is greatness inside of you.

Signed,

Evangelist Ericall Hall

Acknowledgements

First, I would like to acknowledge my Lord and Savior, Jesus Christ, for His grace and mercy. I thank Him for never leaving me nor forsaking me, even when I was at my lowest of lows. I thank Him for being sovereign and long-suffering. I thank Him for being forgiving and trusting me when I didn't trust myself, believing in me when I didn't believe in myself; SEEING THE BEST IN ME, when I just simply could not.

Next, I would like to thank my mother and my father because they are the vessels used to create what exists today. Thank you for directly being my strength, causing me to push past the odds and break through the stereotypical mindsets of those who had painted my future before they even knew my outcome.

Finally, I would like to thank ALL of my family members who carried me through this process called life. Those who stood beside me, behind me, and when I just could not see my way, in front of me and pushed me into destiny. Thank you for the long nights sitting beside me in the hospital, the prayers as my body reeked with pain, the continual support as I made decisions that were not so promising for my life and the many times that bank accounts were exhausted because of my many requests to be involved in something.

Introduction

"If I only knew then, what I know now." How many times, as children, have we heard adults say this in an attempt to teach us right from wrong? How many of us actually listened and took their advice? I'm sure not many of us did. As I share my story, I'd like you to focus on the right that I've done, as well as the wrong and I want you to learn from it. Life is a lot like a roller coaster. It has its ups and downs, but we must realize that there is no struggle too big to overcome. We've been told that God wants us to cast our burdens upon Him. However, we fail to do it because we don't really believe that we can trust Him. We don't believe that He will supply our every need. Instead, we look to man to handle our problems, when oftentimes they are unable to.

I once heard a man of God say, "If He said it, it will come to pass and He tells us in His word that His word won't return void so if we believe, we can have whatever is in His will for our lives." When we ask God for something, we often expect Him to do it immediately, when it may not be time for us to have it. We then become discouraged when things don't work out the way we expected. One truth is our wrongdoings will sometimes block our blessings but regardless of what sins we've committed in the past, we must remember that God is a forgiving God. I thank God that He is not like man. God never leaves our side. If anything, He picks us up and carries us along the way. Always remember, that no matter how you feel about yourself, God has purpose for your life. Accept Him as the head of your life and allow Him to lead and guide you so that you can experience all that He has for you.

Part One:

FAMILY REJECTION

1 Timothy 5:8 "Whoever does not care for his own relatives, especially his own family members, has turned against the faith and is worse than someone who does not believe in God." (NCV)

Allow me to introduce myself and take you on a journey where healing, deliverance and breakthrough took place. I was that little black girl, who from an early age, felt that God had no use for me. I felt I had no reason for being here, no purpose, no nothing. While obstacles were a constant part of my life, pain, confusion, and depression often followed close behind. I was like so many of our youth today. Struggled with peer pressure, experienced love good and bad, and was violated by the very one's I loved and trusted. I want to use my life to inspire today's generation and let them know that it doesn't matter about your past, your hic ups or your mess ups, once you invite Him in, old things are passed away and all things have been made new. You do not have to submit to what the world offers because God has a greater plan for your life. Your latter shall be greater than your past.

Born to a 16-year old teenager in 1981, God already had a plan for my life. He already knew He would make me more powerful than anyone ever thought I could be, as long as my eyes stayed on Him. Yet and still, obstacles and struggles arose as soon as I entered this world; a child being born to a child. Who would take care of whom? Being born into a world where mom was merely a little girl still living at home with her parents, unemployed and rejected by the "baby's daddy", as soon as the words "I'm pregnant" parted from her lips. However, there was a couple that opened their hearts and took me in, although they had kids of their own to raise and care for. I thank God every day because I could have easily became another child in the system but this was not God's plan for my life, and I know that is why He put the necessary people in place to receive me. Not just any people, but God fearing people who would lay my foundation.

Under the care of these great people, who were my grandparents, God begin to do a work in me I would never forget. I moved through the beginning of life unaware of what was going on because I was merely a child without a care. Once of age, I was able to attend school, but I didn't really know what to expect because I felt different and didn't really know why. Remember, my mother was only 16 when she gave birth to me. She was young and inexperienced with caring for herself much less a newborn baby and being raised by my grandparents I felt like an outsider. However, what the enemy meant for bad God turned it around for my good. I went to school and turned out to be one of the smartest kids there

(I'm not bragging but just want you to see how God had favor on my life from the beginning). He loves us because we are His children and He loved me and knew me before I knew myself. His word tells us in Luke 12:7 that He knows the very number of hairs on our heads and we are more valuable than many sparrows, so He had my destiny mapped from the start. No matter what obstacles you've faced in the past, always know God will never leave you or turn His back on you because He is sovereign and just. There were moments when loneliness as young girl would try to creep in but whenever I felt alone or didn't understand why, even as a little girl, I would refer to a poem by an unknown author entitled Footprints.

It reads:

One night a man had a dream. He dreamed he

was walking along the beach with the Lord. Across the sky flashed scenes from his life. For each scene, he noticed two sets of footprints in the sand. One belonged to him and the other to the Lord. When the last scene of his life flashed before him, he looked back at the footprints in the sand. He noticed that many times along the path of his life there was only one set of footprints. He also noticed that it happened at the very lowest and saddest times of his life. This really bothered him and he questioned the Lord about it. "Lord, you said that once I decided to follow you, you'd walk with me all the way. I noticed that during the most troublesome times in my life, there is only one set of footprints. I don't understand why when I needed you the most you would leave me." The Lord replied, "My precious, precious child, I love you and would never leave you. During your time of trial and suffering, when you see only one set of footprints, it was then that I carried you."

After reading this, I would always feel better because it confirmed for me and to me that God was always there. Even when I turn away, He sits patiently waiting with open loving arms ready to receive me just where I am. Take a minute and look back on the times when you were at your lowest. Then think about where you are now. How about the people that called themselves your friends? Did they stay by your side during those low points in your life or did they leave you? Most of the time they were nowhere to be found. You will find that God is the only one that will stick with you no matter what. He says that He is closer than a brother.

I learned from an early age to give everything over to God. My grandmother and aunt always told me, "let go and let God. Let Him fight your battle". I understand that now, but growing up as a teen, it was sometimes difficult to understand. We feel no one understands what we are going through. We are the only one that has to deal with this type of situation. But there is always someone that has experienced and gone through and is willing to see you through. All we have to do is receive Him. He was tempted on EVERY side so there's nothing new to Him. He can bring light to any dark place. He has an army of witnesses standing today that can testify to just that. You WILL make it. You will get to the other side. You will succeed.

I went through the beginning of elementary school with flying colors. I didn't have a care in the world. I lived with my grandparents and had a peaceful life. By the time I was in the third or fourth grade, I had a little brother, who was three years younger than I. I was also living with my mother again. It was at a point where she had decided to again accept her responsibilities as a parent and handle the tasks at hand.

This time we lived in public housing, which was new for me and I felt like we were being punished. I didn't understand why my grandmother would send us back but I knew she was standing on the very faith that she had instilled in me and was giving my mom another chance. But she always coached me through on survival. My grandmother would always tell me to keep to myself and do not get involved with the crowd and I would be okay. She was teaching me then that just because there is turmoil around you, keep your eyes on Him and you will stay afloat. This takes me the story when Peter walked on water. As long as He kept His eyes on Jesus he was ok but just when he started to allow the enemy to distract him and break focus he began to sink. The enemy will try to present every type of distraction to break our focus. But we have to keep our eyes on the promise. It is the promise that holds our blessing and our purpose. My granny positioned me to have a relationship with God at a very early age because she knew what God had before me. She would always say it's not what's on the outside but what's on the inside and you don't have to be a product of your environment. I tried to stand on that very word. I remember asking the Lord, "Why me? Why am I dealing with the back and forth. Why can't we just stay with my grandparents forever and everything be ok? I didn't fully understand. Now looking back I see things differently. Why me has turned into why not me? Jesus suffered and I am surely no better than He. I seemed to forget that God had everything under control and everything happens for a reason and that was merely a season. I didn't know then that God will put you in a season for a reason but soon comes a season change. It doesn't stay winter forever. Spring is soon to come. So I just let it be. In the midst of living with my mom again, our home became the house of the complex. My mom was back under the hold of the enemy, now stronger than ever. I failed to reveal the fact that my mom was a beautiful vessel that had been taken over by the enemy and proved at an early age to weak to break free so my brother and I suffered at the hands of the brokenness. All I knew was to stay in prayer just like I saw my grandmother do all the time. I remember when living with my grandmother I would listen to her walk around the house singing, "This little light of mine, I'm going to let it shine". So I resorted back to what I saw kept her sane in the midnight hour. If it worked for her surely it would work for me because I knew I needed to do something. So as a young child, I stayed before the Lord in hope that it would change something, anything; but I knew to pray and everything would be okay.

One night as I was lying in my bed, still living with my mom, I felt a cool breeze come over me. I didn't really know where the breeze came from considering it was the middle of the summer, but as I slowly opened my eyes there were two men standing over me that I had never seen before. I opened my mouth to scream and nothing came out. I heard one of them say in a faint whisper, "I'll give you a dollar if you let me play with you. I won't hurt you." All I could do was ask the Lord to protect me and wrap me in His Arms. Then all at once I let out a piercing scream from somewhere deep within and they left. This was the final straw for my grandmother, who immediately came and removed us from the home.

I had mixed feelings about this. On one hand I was very happy, but on the other hand I felt like we were neglecting my mother. Although I realized she neglected us long before that, I still loved her. So after a season of living with my grandparents my mom was given another chance and we were sent to live with her again. My grandmother always had hope. She always wanted her to do right and live a life that was pleasing to God and her children but foremost, herself. But unfortunately I found we could only live with her for short periods of time because circumstances always caused us to find ourselves dealing with homelessness. This was hard to deal with. By the time I entered the sixth grade we were living with my grandparents for good. The enemy had completely taken over and what we knew was no longer.

She wasn't there for my first menstrual cycle, my first boyfriend or my first heartbreak. Although there were women in my life whom I truly love and thank God for, it was nothing like sharing these precious moments with my own mother. The pain of not having her in my life was so overwhelming that I suffered an emotional breakdown. It was to the point where my grandmother had to take me to seek psychological help.

There was also the issue of not having a father. I had to admit this was a major issue in my life because I found myself drawn to older men hoping to find that 'missing father figure'. I knew it was a problem, but felt like they gave me the love my father never did. I can remember the days when I would actually hear from my father. He would tell me, "Get your clothes together, I'm on the way" and then I wouldn't hear from him anymore. I would stand at the window all day, waiting for him to pull up. When I'd finally leave the window, every noise I heard would increase my hope of maybe he had shown up after all. No matter how many times he did this to me, I would always forgive him, only to have it start all over again. When he would finally call there would be a million excuses as to why he hadn't shown up. I held anger in my heart towards him for a long time. I had to realize at some point that God does not bless an angry heart and He commands us to forgive. And I couldn't hold anger or hatred because that was simply just not who God had made me to be. He has forgiven me time and time again and I am supposed to do the same.

There are so many people that have and will hurt you, but you must let go and give it to God. My daily quote, "He won't put more on us than we can bear." When people hurt other people, believe you me, they get it back one hundredfold. We may not know when or how and it's not up to us to decide when, but God will take up for His children. He assures us that vengeance is His.

Healing Journal

Part One

_____
_____
_____
_____
_____
_____
_____
_____
_____
_____
_____
_____
_____
_____
_____
_____
_____
_____
_____
_____
_____
_____
_____
_____
_____
_____

PART II:

SOCIAL REJECTION

Psalm 142:4 I look for someone to come and help me, but no one gives me a passing thought! No one will help me; no one cares a bit what happens to me. (NLT)

I learned so many things about myself, especially how to cope without losing my mind. I had already gone through so much already, but I knew God had a plan. My sixth and seventh grade years were manageable once I had direction and stability. I was able to focus in school and didn't have any worries of what I would be presented with once I got home. I was living with my grandparents permanently and things were looking bright. I became a cheerleader and ran track. This allowed me to associate myself with people and have fun. It also kept my mind on positive things. It was exactly what I needed because by the time I hit the eighth grade, I was all smiles on the outside but quicksand on the inside.

My crisis started all over again. This was the year my body was violated. It happened more times than I could count. I felt so numb and low. My body cringed whenever I knew I was going to even be in his presence. When it happened, I couldn't cry or scream. I would just sit in silence thinking to myself, "Lord, please make it stop". I would have moments of complete breakdown. My friends would always tell me, "You're so sensitive. You cry about everything." No one knew the pain I felt inside. I wish the song, "You don't know my story" would have existed back then because they truly did not know my story. I never told anyone what happened to me. I was so embarrassed. I felt unworthy and nasty. It traumatized me to the point I almost failed the eighth grade. I just could not focus anymore in school. I knew if I didn't tell someone, I would snap. So I went to someone who was close to me and I thought would have my back. However, that was not the case. I can still remember the response just like it was yesterday. Their reaction broke my heart and I shut down all over again.

I continued to let this go on until I couldn't take anymore. It was either I hurt them or hurt myself. I really didn't want to hurt anybody so I went to someone else that immediately dealt with the situation. I felt much safer, but knew I had upset that household and wasn't sure what to do about it. After the situation was over, I began to doubt God's love for me. I knew deep in my heart that God could not possibly love me and continue to allow my life to go into a fast plunge of destruction. Or at least I thought! I went back to school and tried to improve my grades. It ended with me barely graduating but I made it.

Slipping back into looking for that manly attention, I had a boyfriend that was graduating from high school and I thought I was grown. Nobody could tell me anything. My boyfriend was 28 and at the time, I didn't know it, but he was sick mentally. This was a grown man dating a little girl. And that little girl was me. Although I was never sexual with him, he felt he owned me. He gave me a pager so he could keep up with me and if he paged and I did not respond, he would snap. I thought it was cute at the time, thinking he did it because he cared about where I was and who I was with. He gave me that attention of a man; making me feel like I mattered and I was important. He was the "man" in my life. It was only cute for so long though. I tried to break up with him and he threatened to shoot my house up. I had to get my family involved and had my god sister's boyfriend beat him up. None of which was godly, but it got the message across.

I had been scared straight. Temporarily……

I finally started high school. Ninth grade, 13 years old and loving every minute of it. My grades were excellent and I had new friends. I had lots of male friends, but nothing serious at first. By the time I reached the end of the ninth grade, I met the man of my dreams. I was in love. Nobody else mattered at the time. We were in our own little world, and although I wasn't allowed to date we talked on the phone day and night. I would sneak out every now and then to see him. We went through the summer very much in love and expressing it every chance we got.

My tenth grade year began, my grades were good and my relationship was still going strong. I was inducted into the National Honor Society, National Vocational Technical Honor Society and Beta Club and my family was very proud of me. I was pleased with my accomplishments and found out soon enough that many didn't share my joy. It was most likely because they were so sure I would fail and became shocked when I hadn't.

I had mentors that always kept me in positive environments. My friends introduced me to a teen Christian organization called, Young Life. My first encounter with the group was a retreat to Windy Gap. I loved it. I was around all these Christian people who were in my age group, but all had different backgrounds and different stories. It made me feel that perhaps my story wasn't quite that bad. I had added positive friends to the friends I already had. It was one of the greatest experiences of my life. It was during this time that God placed two men in my life that would help to shape my future in a very positive way.

Summer time rolled around and life was going well. I had a summer job at the Red Cross and it was nice. I attended church every Sunday with my mentor and we had teen Bible study. I was learning who God was all over again and why He allowed certain things to happen. However, I was not totally in a place where I was ready to commit to Him just yet. I knew He had forgiven me for past sins, but I continued to walk in condemnation. Although I had learned from church and Bible study that God forgives and I should too, I was unable to let some things go.

The time came when it was time to go back to school. Junior year! The excitement of hanging with the upper classmen, attending junior and senior prom and being amongst the elite was almost overwhelming. This was the year I would shine! I was excited. I couldn't wait. We had all we needed to make this a great year. My grandparents always did whatever they could do to make our lives as comfortable as possible considering what we had already been through.

School began and my friends and I walked to school every day. I had finally grown up and life was both comfortable and exciting. I was still going through the boy stage though, still dating the guy from my tenth grade year, off and on. Although he had taken me through hell and high water, he was my first high school love and nothing would ever change that. I also had other male friends that I conversed with. My junior year was the year I had declared to myself and others, that it would be a year of success. I was not going to be a product of my past. School started in August and I was so happy. I had settled well and it was great. I was active in my honors programs and my grades were still good. We had to take the Georgia Graduation test in order to graduate from high school and I passed with flying colors. I knew this would definitely be my year to shine.

By November, chaos was at my door again. I encountered one of the worst experiences of my entire life. Although my body had been violated in the past, it did not compare to what occurred on November 12, 1997. I was 16 years old at the time and I met a guy that was quite older than me. Not sure of the exact age. He was not a student and I later found out he was married and had a little girl. This 'friend' came to pick me up from school to take me to the mall. I was buying a birthday present for my brother. I got in the car, wanting all my friends to see how grown up I made my flesh crawl. He then began to insert his manhood into me and I cried so hard I almost passed out. He never stopped. After he was finish he put my clothes back on and put me in the car. I felt like trash.

He got in the car and drove me home as if we had just shared the most romantic experience ever. The whole time I was crying my eyes out, he kept asking me, "Are you okay?" as if this were all done voluntarily. Then he stopped at the liquor store and asked if I wanted anything. I just wanted to go home. When we got to my house, he dropped me off in the driveway, told me to have a nice day and drove off. I never saw or heard from him again. I felt so nasty and used. I dried my tears, went into the house and got in the shower. I automatically went into a shell. I did not talk to anyone and when I did, I was snappy. I had an attitude with everybody. I didn't want to be bothered. I even turned against my brother, who I loved dearly.

It, of course, affected me in school. My grades dropped and my mood shifted. I remember one of my instructors asking me what was wrong. I told her I was pregnant. She was shocked and asked me what I was going to do. I told her I was having an abortion. She took me in her office and talked to me. I was torn apart when she made me call home. I remember the hurt and disgust in my grandmother's voice when I told her I was about to have a child. She was very upset because my mother had me when she was sixteen and I had already been told over and over again that I would be just like her. These were words that constantly played over and over in my mind. But I had to learn within myself that just because that was the life style of my parents, God's plan for my life was not failure but success. However, at the time I didn't know that because I felt like I would be better accepted if everyone thought I was about to become a teenage parent rather than face the fact that I had just been raped. My grandmother was so upset. And I just cried. I never told anyone because I had heard that date rape was hard to prove. It would be his word against mine and I thought no one would believe me. I felt like it was my fault. Those around me already felt like that was my lifestyle anyway and what better opportunity to provide evidence for the accusation. I felt like that was what people were expecting anyway so I would give them what they wanted.

No one ever came back to ask me what

happened. Was I still pregnant or what happened or who was I pregnant by or when did it even happen? I figured everyone thought I had an abortion. I remember being fussed at so badly. My family was so upset and I could tell very disappointed. Was I about to follow my mother's footsteps? Side note: It doesn't matter what you came from. God has specific destiny and purpose for your life that was established from the day of your conception. He has already mapped out your final destination with all of your mishaps and mistakes already penciled in. You are not a mistake nor are you a failure but you are a blessing created by God to do His will and draw souls to the kingdom. Everything that you have gone through has not been for you, but has been used to strengthen you so that you can reach back and pull your fallen sister or brother up and coach them along the way. (Now back to the regularly scheduled program) I sat at the end of the bed listening and crying, the whole time still not really hearing what was being said. I felt cold and alone. Was it really worth all of this? I felt like it was my fault therefore I never said anything about it. This affected me tremendously. I never brought it up again, but the memory never left me. I began to carry a gun because I felt it would protect me the next time I was faced with that situation. My trust in men was gone. I would never be violated again or someone would die this time. I then took matters into my own hands. All that I stood on, all that I had pulled from watching my grandmother, LEFT! I had to protect me because no one else had seemed to be very successful at it.

While struggling with all the troubles

outside of school, I began to have some serious problems in school. There was a girl there that had become interested in my boyfriend and would do anything to get him. I had officially adopted a bully. She tried to push me over a banister from the third floor. She would bump into me in the hall and constantly try to provoke me. My family had to come up to the school many times as a result of the harassment. It was totally out of control. And I'm not a physical fighter nor have I ever been. I've never had one physical altercation in all my years of life. Thankfully, it was her senior year and she would soon be leaving. That battle would soon be over.

In the midst of, I had a job and a new group of friends. They were my acceptance during my time of unknowing. They led me in a direction I never thought I would ever go, considering I already knew what the outcome would be. I began to smoke cigarettes, which eventually evolved into my smoking weed on a daily basis. I thought I was so cool. I was in the social circle and had been accepted. I had my friends at school and for some reason I just didn't feel a part of the "in" crowd, but it was nothing like being cool on the streets. It brought about a different kind of acceptance. I felt as if I were living a double life. My family knew nothing of it. However, after a while, I just didn't feel right. I knew what the streets and drugs did to my parents and I refused to let my life go down the drain like that. Although I had convinced myself God had no purpose for my life, my family constantly reminded me that He did and God constantly reminded me through all of my school accomplishments and the mere fact that He allowed me to see day after day after day.

I faced hardships, but overall I survived. Satan tried to attack, but I knew there were prayers being sent out for me every day and God was answering them. We will be hit with problems in the world, but we can't let them overpower us, putting us in a place where we want to give up. God allows us to go through to make us stronger. Going into my senior year, I was both nervous and anxious. Nervous because I made it to my final year of high school transitioning into semi adulthood and anxious because the bullying phase of my life was finally over and now I was able to have a normal school year. I was excited about what was to come. I had a new boyfriend and he was a good guy. However, because of the blows that life dealt me, I was unable to recognize the good in him and instead focused on the bad.

Healing Journal

Part Two

_____
_____
_____
_____
_____
_____
_____
_____
_____
_____
_____
_____
_____
_____
_____
_____
_____
_____

PART III:

ROMANTIC REJECTION

Song of Solomon 1:2 *Let him kiss me with the kisses of his mouth— for your love is more delightful than wine.* (NIV)

This began a revolving cycle in my life that overtook me. I became so displeased with myself, believing that I wasn't normal and that there must be something wrong with me. I began to abuse myself to suppress the low self-esteem, hurt, heartache, and depression, feelings of neglect, abuse, rape and molestation. I abused myself by abusing my body. I became very promiscuous because it was all I knew to bandage the pain. Although my aunt was a strong female figure in my life, it just didn't fill the emptiness of not having a mother or father to call my own. I realized that not having a father figure in my life caused me to allow men to use and abuse me from early childhood. Seeking men for love, I became involved for all the wrong reasons. I wanted a void filled that only God could fill but at the time I didn't understand. I felt like my body was all that I had to offer and by offering it they would stay and not leave me because of the cliché, all men want is sex anyway. So why not satisfy his desire and in turn allow him to see my greatness and want to stay and love me. I knew that I was being categorized as a whore, but I was merely yearning to be loved. When we find ourselves seeking and searching and in a place where we have allowed the enemy to redirect our focus we begin to compromise our self-worth, our self-love and our self-respect. Thus finding myself in a place where I didn't see myself the way everyone else saw me. I figured if I gave these men what they wanted, perhaps one of them could actually love me past the sex. My mindset was if I slept with him, he'd know I'm for real and want to be with me and in turn fill that empty void.

After a while, I began to realize that I

had no idea what real love was. I didn't love myself so how could I love someone else. And how could I expect someone to love me if I didn't. Men had hurt me so much that I didn't know how to get to a place that I allowed a man to truly love me. It was after this realization that I began to question my sexuality. I didn't believe a man could ever really love me, so I decided to switch lanes. However, God stepped in and ended that before it ever began. I found myself having the desires and the curiosity but could never fully put it into drive. I then found myself once again facing my old buddies – loneliness and confusion. It didn't help that I also had low self-esteem. I was so skinny and lanky all my life. I watched as the "thick" girls got all the compliments and the popular boys sashayed around them as if they were top of the line. I felt I was beneath them. I was not being accepted because I wasn't thick and I didn't have a big butt with wide hips and large breasts. I felt like they couldn't love me but in actuality they weren't supposed to. I wasn't in a place to be loved by man because I had not placed myself in a place to understand the love that I was receiving from my heavenly man every day. His love is the first love. He is the only One that completely loves you past, through, and in spite of. Man can always come in and satisfy the flesh but when your spirit has received a pure touch from Daddy, that fleshly satisfaction becomes null and void. You will find yourself in a place where your first thought is – do our spirits connect? Not how fine is he, or I'll sleep with him to keep him, or get pregnant and maybe he'll stay (That was for somebody). Babies won't make them stay – in most cases it only makes them go away.

Well, graduation day finally arrived. The time had come for all of life's decisions to meet in one place and lead me on the path that God had mapped out from the beginning. June 9, 1999 marked my transition in adulthood. Where would I go from here? My parents did not come, but my family did. And I was just as appreciative as they were proud. I knew that taking a break as others said they were going to do would not be a good idea so I began college in August of 1999. By the time I began, the enemy had presented himself again. Due to some complications in my body I had to withdraw from school. I was very hurt. This was my time. I had overcome trials and tribulations beyond my control and I was ready to move forward with life. In 2000 I was diagnosed with severe endometriosis and double female reproductive organs. This caused day to day activities to become tasking. I had my first laparoscopy in April of 2000 and another in April of 2001. I was told I would have to have numerous miscarriages before I could have children because my double uterus was not large enough to carry a baby full term.

August of 2001, I became pregnant for the very first time. This was my only pregnancy. I did not find out until I was 14 weeks pregnant because all tests came back negative. My body wasn't registering that I was pregnant; however, the ultrasound confirmed it. There were a lot of complications and at five and a half months, I dilated one centimeter and was told my cervix was too weak to carry full term. The doctors advised the baby's father and I to accept the fact that the pregnancy would terminate. However, God had another plan and with His grace, I carried a healthy baby boy to 39 weeks. The doctors were baffled and we were advised against ever trying to have another baby. I'm not condoning premarital sex, nor am I uplifting my having a baby out of wedlock but I am saying that He can take our mistakes and use them for the glory of the Kingdom. What the enemy means for our bad, He uses the very situation to strengthen us and take us higher. Now I can look back and tell that young single mother, IF HE DID IT FOR ME, SURELY HE WILL DO IT FOR YOU! It's not the end of the world. Use that stumbling block as a mere lesson learned and push forward. Don't look down on yourself and don't look at it as a disappointment. God uses all situations for His glory. And you are STILL special in His eye.

In February 2002, while carrying this very same child, my paternal grandmother died, never seeing her first great grand. That was very hard for me and stressful on my body and I almost went into labor the day I walked into her hospital room for the last time and witnessed her dying. We buried her on Feb. 13, 2002. I was seven months pregnant and on complete bed rest, but during her illness, I pressed to be at her side. I had always been by her side through the sickness and visited her often in the hospital. I was even by her side the day she had her leg amputated and spending time in her home during the healing process. This was hard but I knew the love I had for her and felt it my duty to be there during the heavy times. And I am appreciative to have had the opportunity to be there when it mattered most.

Healing Journal

Part Three

_____
_____
_____
_____
_____
_____
_____
_____
_____
_____
_____
_____
_____
_____
_____
_____
_____
_____
_____

PART IV:

BLESSED REJECTION

Isaiah 54:17 No weapon that is formed against thee shall prosper; and every tongue that shall rise against thee in judgment thou shalt condemn. This is the heritage of the servants of the LORD, and their righteousness is of me, saith the LORD. (KJV)

My son Jharis was born in May 2002 and was healthy. The report of the doctor was not received and therefore did not manifest. Whose report did I believe? The report of the Lord! The enemy couldn't kill him in the womb although he tried to get me to accept it thus giving it power to manifest. But I didn't and so he tried to attack his body with sickness after birth. He was not fond of eating and his doctor wanted to put him in the hospital. He had severe asthma with two episodes of pneumonia. This is when my faith began to increase quickly and I found myself in a place where I had relinquished full control to God and asked him to have His way in my life and my son's life. The word tells us that with His stripes we were healed which let me know the enemy had no territorial authority over my son's health and I had to snatch him back. My son never went into the hospital and he grew out of his asthma.

Although I had my son at age 21, out of wedlock, I still felt blessed. God had spared his life after the doctors had counted him out. I finally had something of my own and his father was also an incredible person who needed to see Gods hand at work. But I wasn't completely free. As happy as I was on the outside, I was still very unhappy on the inside. As a result, I ended up hurting my child's father because the love from a man was foreign to me. I wasn't doing it on purpose; I couldn't help it. I had developed a mentality of "I will hurt you before you hurt me." He, like so many others that crossed my path, did not deserve this. Genuine love was not familiar to me and I couldn't recognize it because of my past. I had absolutely no idea how to recognize when real love was present because I felt like it was few and far.

I started taking antidepressants to deal with the depression and pain but quickly noticed an alternate effect that they had. They were causing me to gain weight and when I realized they caused weight gain I had to have them. For the first time I felt like I had become physically appealing and was turning heads! I felt accepted because I was sexy and beautiful. I eventually became addicted to anti-depressants. I went from not loving myself to not loving myself plus drawing the wrong attention. This new weight gain attracted more men, which lead to more sex, more unsuccessful relationships and more ungodly soul ties; which only succeeded in creating more unhappiness, heartache, heartbreak, depression, pain and still, in the end, not loving myself. It was a vicious cycle that I didn't know how to break.

I can recall as a preteen having episodes where I would sit in the corner at home and cry and yell that no one loved me because that's how I felt. I remember being drawn to any older woman that showed me attention because I longed for that mother figure, so everyone's mother became my mother. Rejection was something that I had always felt. I never felt accepted by certain people around me. I felt that I was always looked upon as being less fortunate, making me a charity case. I was the skinny dark skinned little girl with the coarse hair. I felt like the ugly duckling; always seeking attention but not receiving it caused anger, hurt, and disappointment in my life.

My life began to change for the better when I started attending Cornerstone of Faith

COGIC in June 2002. This was when I had my oldest son Jharis, and he was approximately four or five weeks old. My best friend attended the church and she invited me to go with her. Being raised Baptist, attending a COGIC church was a new experience for me. My son and I attended one Sunday and I had the Pastor pray for him regarding his appetite and his situation immediately changed. He never had to be hospitalized and his appetite increased immediately. I knew then I was home. Dr. Taylor believed in me and entrusted me with ministry because he saw the call and the gift. I was a praise dancer, an administrator and an intercessor and he allowed me to work freely as God wanted me to. I received a lot of wisdom and impartation from him. I looked at him as my spiritual father. He was there whenever I needed him even if it was just a shoulder to cry on. I remember there was a season in my life where I wanted to completely throw in the towel and walk away. I shared this with my youth pastor, whom I administrated for, and I told my aunt. I didn't have the heart to tell him however, the word got out.

    I remember being at a community day event at the church and him simply saying those few words no one wanted to hear, "I need to talk to you in my office after the event." I just smiled and said ok. We went into the sanctuary and he asked me what was going on and we talked. However, his final words stuck with me. He said, "You are a lot like me. We've faced situations early in life that forced us into adulthood and because of that we had to grow up early. It caused us to be strong and independent and put us in a place where people depended on us. WE CAN'T AFFORD TO GIVE UP! We have too much that depends on us making it. When we see ourselves giving up, we get right back in line because we have never had the option of giving up." Those words stood with me because it made me think of all the times where I wanted to give up but couldn't and didn't.

One of the times I can recall was when I was facing a lot of adversity from women in the church because I dated one of the ministers prior to us both joining the church and working in ministry side-by-side. I went through a lot of heartache and embarrassment due to relational decisions I made. I never blamed God or gave credit to the enemy. I've learned some things we bring on ourselves by making decisions not confirmed by God. I also learned that elevation sometimes comes with shame and embarrassment. He will prepare a table before our enemies and in 2009 that's exactly what He did. All those that spoke against me and released negativity over my life, had to eat their own words, because He took me from amongst them and sat me before them, so His Glory could shine. God showed me I had become a household name for those that were around me.

I was put where some desired to be and accepted it all with humility and thanksgiving. Cornerstone of Faith was where my rebirth took place. Going through the adversity really hurt me. It was embarrassing but public shame brought public elevation, I thought. In 2009 I received two different words about becoming a First Lady. The first came from a prophet that ministered at the church. I was told that my spirit was humble and that God had equipped me to be a First Lady. Shortly after, I was walking through the grocery store and an older guy approached me. He asked me if I was coming from church, and I told him that I was. He asked if I was married, and at the time I wasn't. He was a minister in his church and was seeking a wife although I wasn't the one of choosing for him. After expressing my lack of interest his final words to me were, "the next time I see you I want you to be a pastor's wife because that is what you are called to be." He said my dress, demeanor and what he felt in my spirit, equipped me for the call he saw on me. I looked at this sent word in two ways: As a confirmation to a prophecy received and an answer to a prayer released. God said His word would not return to Him void and that was destiny being spoken over me, but I didn't really understand what I was being called into.

It's funny because people say Internet dating is not of God. However, if I were not on the Internet, then God could not have honored my now, ex-husband's request, by putting me in a place for him to find me. My ex-husband has a heart and life sold out for Christ. He also has a passion for the youth, as do I. The Holy Spirit recognized that we were equally yoked. I saw my ex-husband advertising his events for the youth through a youth conference and I contacted him first for ministry. I was the youth administrator for my church at the time. We exchanged words and he invited me to a revival a church was having, where he was the MC. I told him I would have on red and black so he would know who I was and when I got there the ENTIRE guest church had on red and black! It was hilarious! However, he said he knew exactly who I was. After we were married

I asked him when he knew I was his wife, and he jokingly answered "When you walked in wearing that pencil skirt, I KNEW!" We began dating and ten months later, on November 30, I was Mrs. McCoy.

I faced a lot of obstacles from the beginning because I married into a house that had gotten comfortable with being raised by a single father. So when momma came in, the grounds were shaken and I was not welcomed. I had women performing witchcraft against me. I had people upset because they felt I did not fit the ministry. I had people that thought I was too weak because of what they saw on the outside and never took the time to know me as a person and a woman of God. There were people that didn't like me because I shook up solid ground. There were even those that just felt like I was NOT his wife and that he belonged to them. So my obstacles were far from few. I watched as some single handedly tried to destroy my marriage. I faced opposition and rebellion from members when trying to lead auxiliaries. I even went through a season when I felt like my husband had a "customer service" mentality in the church, with a motto, "My members are always right and they do no wrong". I experienced a period in my life where a slothful spirit had overtaken me because I was also facing adversity in my marriage and wasn't focusing on ministry, nor did I want to. Primarily because I knew it made him happy and I didn't want to do anything to make him happy if I wasn't happy with what he was doing and how he was doing it. I felt like I was being asked to compromise my identity and not be who God made me to keep HIM happy, so I was labeled as not being the ideal choice by the people.

I went through a phase in my life where I felt alone. Couldn't talk to the women around me because some had motifs to destroy my marriage or create an atmosphere for me to fail and I couldn't tarnish the man of God or the ministry. Couldn't talk to my husband because I felt like in his mind I was inadequate and a disappointment. So God pushed me into a corner on my knees and made me realize that all I had was Him. When the realization hit me that all I needed was Him, then He began to answer my prayer requests one by one. I had to get to the place where I looked to Him and Him alone. Psalm 121 became my place of reference when all else seemed hopeless:

> [1]I will lift up mine eyes unto the hills, from whence cometh my help. [2]My help

cometh from the LORD, which made heaven and earth. ³He will not suffer thy foot to be moved: he that keepeth thee will not slumber. ⁴Behold, he that keepeth Israel shall neither slumber nor sleep. ⁵The LORD is thy keeper: the LORD is thy shade upon thy right hand. ⁶The sun shall not smite thee by day, nor the moon by night. ⁷The LORD shall preserve thee from all evil: he shall preserve thy soul. ⁸The LORD shall preserve thy going out and thy coming in from this time forth, and even for evermore.

And through this, healing began to take place. I began to understand things about myself when I let Him in and put Him first. I was not whole when I married and man could not complete me. I needed to be a whole person, so I could be the leader God needed me to be and bring wholeness to others. When two people come together to join in unity they must be whole to receive the oneness expressed in the Word. If they are not whole themselves, then you merely have two halves, or two incomplete people joining to create chaos and confusion. I prayed and asked God for strategy to fix the shortfalls and weak areas in my life and He sent to me two dynamic women for healing and development. One was a Pastor and she opened my eyes to some deeply rooted issues and brought light to dark places. We were able to give issues and spirits names and put the blood of Jesus on them. The second was an Apostle and she came in afterwards further revealing even more issues, developing me into the intercessor, mother, woman of God, and eventually the Pastor's wife God called me to be to thus advancing the Kingdom. . I learned in this process that you have to be your husband's best friend by encouraging him, protecting him in the spirit and respecting him as your husband, but as a man of God first. I learned to listen without judgment. I learned how to reprove and rebuke in love. Proverbs 31:12: She does him good and not evil all the days of her life. I've learned to declare and decree.

However, I quickly found that when there aren't two fighting vessels that are *willing* to fight and hold on at the same time this gives strength and control to the enemy. This Apostle shared several golden nuggets for me to hold on to allowing me to be victorious in all that I go through. I've learned that marriage is designed to kill you. It kills every ungodly mindset, every ungodly action, and every ungodly thought pattern. It makes us see characteristics in ourselves that we may not see if we were single because relationships come with humbling and compromising one's self. And if you're not prepared for your coming out party, you'll find yourself confused, lost and in an unwavering state of mind.

That's why in prayer being specific when praying for a spouse is imperative. We pray for the things we want and neglect to express the things we don't want. Its two fold. Create a complete package for God to deliver. And also pray that He prepares you for your request. But in God restructuring me and continuing to set me up for greatness, He allowed one final situation to take place. March 2012 was a month and year that brought about a lot of emotions and questions and changed my life forever. I saw my promise crumble before me. That thing that I had prayed for, that purpose that had been fulfilled, that answered prayer was no longer. My divorce was final. It's something when you know you have sought God for something that you received only to see it taken away at the blink of an eye. And you'll never fully understand why.

It's not always easy, and a number of times I have wanted to throw in the towel, but until God's purpose is fulfilled in my life, I don't have the right to abort the mission. He has blessed me with purpose and not only one blessed child, but two. Two beautiful sons that doctors said should not be here. Just for the record and to further let you know how God has blessed again DESPITE, when he blessed me with my second son in January 2011 I went through a lot of sickness and pain and at the end he was caught in the umbilical cord causing an emergency C-section to take place. BUT the blessing at the end was worth it all. He has breath in his lungs and health in his body.

I look back over my life and realize people really don't know my story. I am thankful that through the washing in His Holy blood I don't look like what I've been through. God has seen the best in me from the beginning. Even when man belittled me and I didn't love myself.

So many times in life we go through trials and tribulations not fully understanding why. However, with growth you begin to understand that there is purpose in the process. How many situations have we went through that we know should have taken us out but with His strength we are still standing today? How many times have we been rejected for a job only to get a better one? Or been rejected by a mate or a person of interest only to get someone better? There are times you won't fully understand the rejection and at times you just shouldn't try but you must push knowing with God on your side He won't leave you nor forsake you. Through the pain, the disappointment, and the setbacks walk like the King / Queen you are destined and called to be. Stand knowing that only what you do for Christ will last, and know that all of your rejection is blessed. It is blessed because if HE would not have allowed rejection to take place then we would not have been positioned to receive what He has for you and us.

THE END RESULT OF REJECTION IS GREATNESS!

Healing Journal

Part Four

_____
_____
_____
_____
_____
_____
_____
_____
_____
_____
_____
_____
_____
_____
_____
_____
_____
_____

Epilogue

As I come to the end of what seems like a life of ups and downs coupled with lessons learned, I pray "Blessed Rejection" creates the opening for you to walk into your tomorrow. It was and is my prayer that the journey through my life has paved a way for those who decided to join me to see and understand there is light on the other side. Despite what it looks like, it doesn't have to stay that way and your latter will be greater than your past.

Drowned in my own hiccups, I almost missed the opportunity given by God to celebrate my survival and provide a survival guide for those to come. When He gave me the title "Blessed Rejection" it was during a time of healing. And it was given with a peace that surpassed any level of understanding that I could have had. No matter how dark and gloomy it looked, the rejection was just a setback that set me apart for my setup. Thus creating an atmosphere where growth and elevation in Him has taken place. And with that the birthing of a woman that is moving forward, pressing toward and looking upward because in the end a "Refined Woman" has been birthed..........

Coming Soon!!!!!!!!

Discussion Questions:

1. Has life presented you with situations where you felt rejected? What feelings did that rejection stir up? How did you deal with this or these situation(s)?
2. Which type of rejection do you feel has most affected God's plan for your life?
3. Do you feel like one type of rejection is worse than the next? Why or why not?
4. Does rejection seem to affect males or females worse? Tell why?
5. Does rejection leave unforgettable and unforgivable residue?
6. What have you learned from your personal experiences of dealing with rejection?

7. Have you ever felt God's presence while feeling like you were going through rejection in some area? If so, explain?
8. How did He renew, refresh and redirect you into wholeness?
9. Do you feel like dealing with rejection caused you to be a better person? If so, explain.
10. What is your view on greatness being the result of all of your past trials and tribulations?

www.ingramcontent.com/pod-product-compliance
Lightning Source LLC
Chambersburg PA
CBHW051700090426
42736CB00013B/2462